THE ORGANIC HANDBOOK 7

BEDS

Labour-saving, space-saving, more productive gardening

Pauline Pears

Henry Doubleday Research Association / Search Press

First published in Great Britain 1992
Search Press Ltd.,
Wellwood, North Farm Road,
Tunbridge Wells, Kent TN2 3DR

in association with

The Henry Doubleday Research Association,
National Centre for Organic Gardening,
Ryton-on-Dunsmore,
Coventry CV8 3LG

Illustrations by Polly Pinder
Photographs by Charlotte de la Bedoyère
All the photographs in this book have been taken in organic
gardens, and all the fruit, vegetables and flowers pictured have
been grown organically. The Publishers would like to thank
the HDRA for the photographs of beds on pages 6 and 24.

Distributed in Canada by

Cavendish Books Inc.,
Unit 5, 801 West 1st. Street,
North Vancouver, BC. V7P1A4

ISBN 0 85532 697 2

*To Ned, who shares my beds, and to the
many HDRA members who wrote in with
their own 'bedtime stories'.*

Conversion chart

From centimetres to inches		From grams to ounces	
1 cm	= ½ in	7 g =	¼ oz
2.5 cm	= 1 in	14 g =	½ oz
5 cm	= 2 in	28 g =	1 oz
10 cm	= 4 in	110 g =	4 oz
50 cm	= 20 in	450 g =	16 oz (1 lb)
100 cm (1 m)	= 40 in	*From litres to pints*	
1 sq m	= 1.2 sq yds	1 l = 1.75 pt	

Exact conversions from imperial to metric measures
are not possible, so the metric measures have been
rounded up.

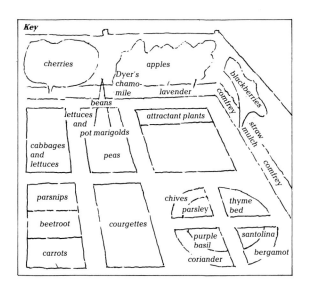

Composition by Genesis Typesetting, Rochester, Kent
Printed in Spain by Elkar S. Coop

Introduction

In a bed garden the ground is divided up into individual beds of such a shape and size that they do not need to be walked on. All sowing, weeding, planting and harvesting is done from the path that surrounds each bed.

This approach may not sound revolutionary, but it can have quite a dramatic effect on your gardening methods and the results that you achieve. The main difference is in vegetable growing. Because there is no need to leave space to walk on between the rows, plants can be closely spaced and distributed evenly over the growing area. This results in higher yields, even when the area used for paths is taken into account. The space between plants can be adjusted to control the size of each individual, producing made-to-measure vegetables! Some gardeners use beds just for vegetables. Others convert their whole garden, using beds to grow fruit, flowers and herbs as well as vegetables.

Some advocates of bed gardening recommend regular deep digging which raises the soil level, hence the name 'raised' or 'deep' beds. The title of this book does not include either of these terms, as it deals with all sorts of beds, from 'double dug' to 'never dug'.

The organic approach to gardening is followed in this book. Composts, manures and other organic materials, together with good management techniques, are used to build soil fertility. Weeds are controlled by mulching and cultivation. Plants are kept healthy by making the soil fertile, encouraging natural predators and by using a whole range of other organic methods.

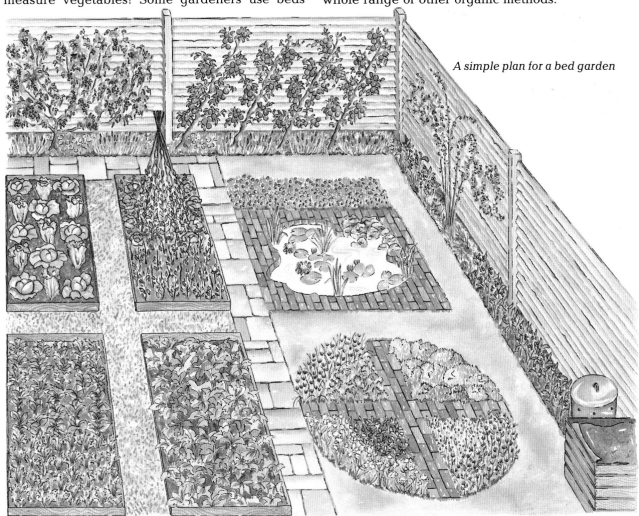

A simple plan for a bed garden

3

Reaching to the middle of a 1.25m wide bed is easy, even for children

Advantages of beds

If you are used to gardening on an open plot, then the idea of dividing the ground up into narrow beds about 1.25m wide, with a path around each, might sound rather strange, not to mention a waste of valuable space. However, many gardeners who have taken to growing on beds would not have it any other way.

● **Higher yields** Despite the space taken up by access paths around each bed, this system of growing will produce more from the total area of ground than a 'conventional' system. Because the beds are not walked on, plants can be grown more closely than usual, so more can be fitted into the space.

● **Less work** With the ground divided up into several individual beds, tasks such as weeding or digging become more manageable, and you can experience the satisfaction of finishing a whole

bed in a relatively short time. With a bed system it is only the growing area that is cultivated and fed. In a conventional system the whole area is prepared, and then it is compacted again by walking over it, leaving large areas between rows unused (except by weeds).

● **Easier for beginners and children** Several small beds are much easier for beginners to manage than a large plot. Also, the division between paths and beds is very obvious, so children find it easier to tell where they should and should not walk.

● **Good for stiff backs** If you find bending difficult and spend most of your time gardening on your knees, then a bed system is the answer. Where the beds have sturdy edgings you can sit on them, again avoiding the need for so much bending.

- **Easy weeding** Close planting means that many weeds are smothered out. A single weeding may be all that is needed for leafy crops such as carrots. Weeds that do grow can be pulled out easily.

- **Easy viewing** Organic gardeners should always keep a watchful eye on their plants to prevent problems developing. Plants are more accessible and, thus, easier to view when grown in blocks on a bed system.

- **Rotation simplified** It is much easier to plan and keep track of a crop rotation system when the ground is divided up into permanent beds.

- **Good for poor soils** If your garden will not grow much because, for example, the soil is just builders' rubble and subsoil or the topsoil is very shallow, then a bed system is ideal. A fertile soil can be built on top of the poor soil, rather than attempting the major task of improving it downwards.

- **Control over crop size** The traditional spacing recommended for vegetables tends to produce plants that are too large for many households. The even spacing used on a bed system can be adjusted to provide any size of vegetable that you require.

- **Earlier cropping** On beds, the soil tends to be lighter and less compacted, so it warms up more quickly in the spring and plants start to grow earlier.

- **Protected cropping** When plants are grown in widely spaced rows very few will fit under a cloche. Because there are many more plants to the square metre on a bed system, one cloche can protect more plants.

- **Intercropping and companion planting** If you like to grow flowers and vegetables together, then it is easy to dot a few flowers among the vegetables, or vice versa, when the plants are evenly spaced over the bed. Different plants can also be grown together for the purpose of pest control.

- **Good for small quantities** Beds are usually about 1.25m wide. This means that rows of flowers and vegetables need only be 1.25m long, which is more practical for the solo gardener than a conventional long-rowed plot.

- **More gardening days** Beds can be weeded, planted and harvested on rainy days when a conventional plot would be too wet to walk on.

Close planting of leafy crops, such as carrots, reduces the need for weeding

An example of growing large cabbages on a bed. These ones are protected by a fine mesh netting to exclude butterflies.

Tomatoes and cabbages grown in alternate rows for pest control   *young plants mature plants*

5

Planning the layout

It is worth taking some time and trouble to plan your bed garden before getting down to work. Although it is not disastrous if you get it wrong the first time around, the beds and paths are intended to be relatively permanent and reorganizing them can take some effort. Squared paper, a pencil, a ruler, and a pair of compasses (for more elaborate shapes) are needed to draw the plans. A good tape measure, lots of sticks and some string are required for laying out the design on the ground.

Measuring up

You may be converting your whole garden, or just a part of it, to beds. Whatever the case, your first task is to measure up your site and draw out a plan of it on a piece of squared paper.

The beds

The next step is to decide on the shape, size and layout of the beds.

Shape
Bed gardens can be all sorts of shapes and sizes, as long as you can always reach to the middle of the bed from the path.

If you are converting a conventional vegetable plot, then a set of rectangular beds may be a good choice as they are simple to lay out and to manage. In a small garden you may prefer to create a more imaginative design, which looks attractive and grows a mixture of edible and ornamental plants.

Elaborately shaped beds can have odd corners which are difficult to cultivate and may not suit the

Raised beds in a simple rectangular plan. Some of the beds contain grazing rye and others contain strawberries.

larger vegetable crops. The first problem can be overcome by using a no-dig system (see pages 15–17). The second problem can be solved by using the elaborate beds for flowers, herbs and smaller vegetables, and creating some simple rectangular beds on which to grow the larger vegetables.

Dimensions

Width

Beds should be of a width that enables you to work on them comfortably from the path. The general recommendation is that they should be not more than 1.25m wide. Provided that this width suits you it is useful to keep to it, as manufacturers are beginning to produce cloches, netting and other crop covers to fit this size of bed. If you have not used a bed system before, then mark out a strip 1.25m wide and try it out. If, for example, you find that you cannot reach to plant out a row of beans up the middle of the bed, then reduce the width until you can.

Where space is limited, do not make the beds too narrow as this increases the proportion of ground used as paths. Where a bed is bounded on one side by a wall or a fence, it should be about half the width of the others.

Orientation

If you are able to choose which way the beds run in your garden, then aim for the length of the bed to run north/south, or as near north/south as possible. This means that all the plants should get the same amount of sunshine.

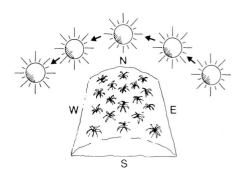

The whole bed receives sunshine

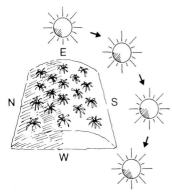

The plants on one side of the bed will tend to shade the other side

Length

In theory, a bed can be as long as the size of your garden or plot will allow, but, for various reasons, it is sensible to limit the length.

● When a bed is empty you should not walk on it, and when it is full you will not be able to walk on it or jump over it. It is a long walk to the other side if you are half-way down a 10m bed. If you are tempted to step on the beds to reach the other side, then build yourself a mobile bridge.

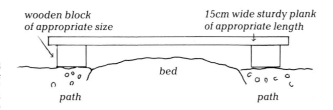

wooden block of appropriate size   15cm wide sturdy plank of appropriate length

bed

path   path

• If you are growing vegetables using a crop rotation, then it is easier to have four or eight short beds than to have just a couple of long ones.

The beds need not all be of the same length. You might make short ones for flowers or herbs and longer ones for vegetables. If you use a crop rotation, then make sure that for each part of the rotation the total length of bed is equal.

The paths

The paths are just as important as the beds. They may look like a waste of growing space, but because of the intensive cropping on the beds they are not, and it is not worth skimping on them unless you are extremely fit and agile.

Points to consider:

• How narrow a path can you work from? The minimum is probably 30cm, but if you are not very supple and need to kneel rather than squat to work then 45–50cm would be more practical. There is no point in being uncomfortable.

• A wheelbarrow will need a wider path, approximately 60cm. You may choose to have some wide paths for wheelbarrow access, alternating with narrower paths. If you are happy to carry fork loads of manure from the ends of the beds, then you will only need wide ones at the ends.

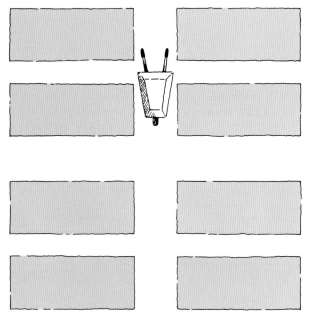

Wide paths allow wheelbarrow access

Remember that a fully laden wheelbarrow needs a reasonable width of path to turn a corner without depositing its load onto the ground.

Compost space

When you are converting a whole garden to beds, remember to leave adequate space for compost heaps, manure and leaf mould. This could be an area set aside for the purpose. Alternatively, you may decide to move the heaps from bed to bed over the years, so that all can benefit from the goodness that will seep out into the soil.

Drawing the plan

Having considered the basic points, the next stage is to decide what you want. Before getting to work on the ground, cut your beds out of paper, to the same scale as your garden plan, and try them for size. This will enable you to explore and compare different patterns before making a final decision. To give you some ideas, a variety of different layouts are illustrated overleaf.

Once you are happy with your layout on paper, you can then mark out the beds on the ground. The following information should help you both to draw up your plans accurately on paper and lay out the final designs on the ground.

Marking out a square

On paper

Use squared paper, where squares are already marked out.

On the ground

1. Mark out one side of the bed (A-B) with two sticks and a length of string.
2. Find something with a right-angled corner to set the position of the second side (A-C). This could be a home-made plywood template, or you could try using the corner of a sheet of paper.
3. Repeat the process at the other two corners (C and D).

Marking out a rectangle

On paper

Use squared paper.

On the ground

Follow the instructions for marking out a square, but extend two opposite sides to the required length.

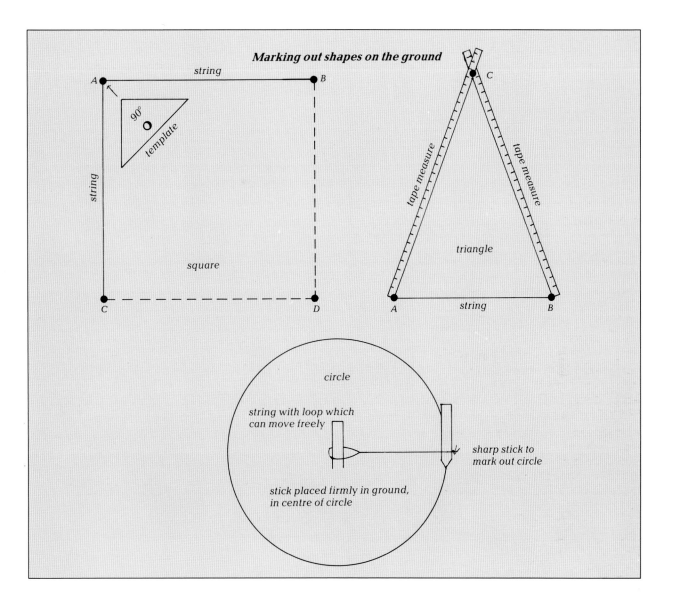

Marking out shapes on the ground

Marking out a triangle

On paper

Using a pair of compasses:
1. Draw the base of the triangle (A-B).
2. Set the compasses to the length of the other two sides of the triangle. Place the point of the compasses at A and mark an arc. Do the same at B. The top of the triangle is where the arcs cross.

On the ground

1. Mark out the base with string (A-B). Attach one tape measure to A and another one to B.
2. Bring the two tapes together, to meet where they mark the correct length of the sides of the triangle. This is the third point of the triangle (C).

Marking out a circle

On paper

Use a pair of compasses, or a circular object such as an egg-cup.

On the ground

1. Hammer a stick firmly into the ground at the point where the centre of the circle is to be.
2. Loosely attach a length of string to the stick, so that the string can move round freely.
3. Tie a sharp stick to the other end of the string, at a distance half the width of the circle.
4. Keeping the string taut, move in a circle round the central post, scraping the ground with the sharp stick.
5. If necessary, the circle scraped by the stick can then be marked with sand to give a clearer line.

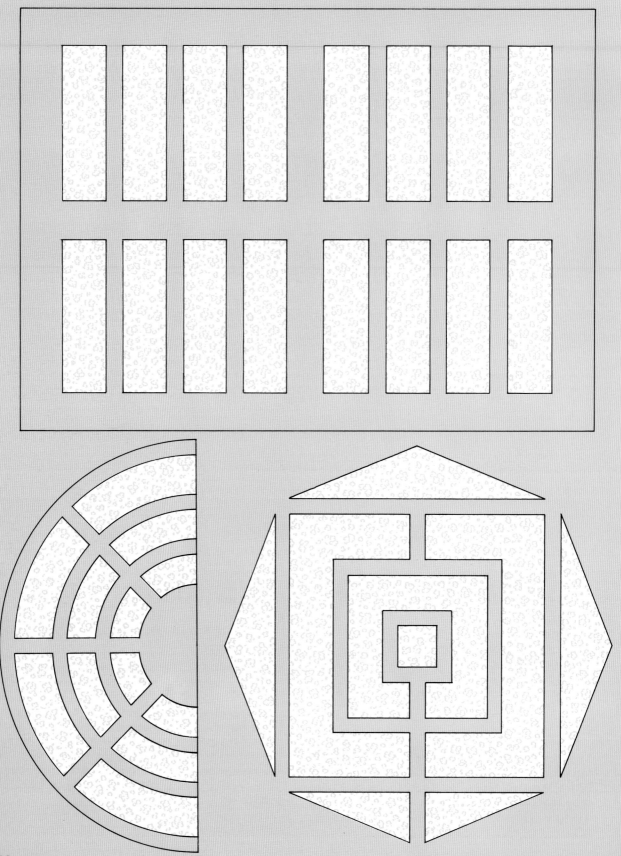

11

Preparing the site

If you are making beds on a piece of land that you have not used before, then this section is for you. However, if you know the soil already, then you can move on to the section on choosing your beds.

Know your soil

When taking over a plot for the first time, find out as much as you can about the soil. This can help you to work out how best to care for it and save you disappointment in the future. If the drainage is poor, fertility is low, or the pH is wrong, then now is the time to deal with it.

Soil type

Different types of soil should be managed in different ways. To work out your soil type, rub some moist topsoil between your fingertips. A soil that is predominantly sand feels gritty; silt feels smooth, almost like talcum powder; and clay feels sticky. Now try moulding the soil; roll some into a ball, then into a cylinder, and see if this will bend into a ring. A very sandy soil will not even form a ball, whereas clay is easily formed into a ring, and silt will form a weak ring. If you wish, then you can have your soil type identified professionally.

Managing clay and silty soils

- Never dig when the soil is too wet or too dry.
- Avoid walking on the soil.
- These soils are rarely short of plant foods, but they need plenty of organic matter to improve the structure.

- To prevent the soil from capping, add fine compost or leaf mould to seed-beds and use it to cover seed drills.
- In spring use cloches to warm the soil, or raise early crops indoors.

Managing sandy soils

- Add plenty of organic matter to improve the structure and help water retention.
- Dig only when absolutely necessary.
- Mulch to stop water loss.
- Shortage of plant foods is often a problem. Use compost, manure and, if necessary, organic fertilizers.

Soil structure and profile

Dig a square hole, about 50cm deep. The sides of the hole will show a 'profile' of the soil. Take a good look at it.

Good signs are:
- A deep layer of dark topsoil.
- Plenty of air channels and earthworm burrows.
- Long branching roots on any plants present.

Bad signs are:
- A topsoil that is very crumbly or stays in hard lumps even when moist.

Action Add organic matter.

- A hard layer of compacted soil, known as a pan, some way below the soil surface.

Action Break up this layer by digging.

- Shallow topsoil over thick clay, chalk, builders' rubble.

Clay soil

Sandy soil

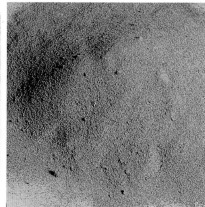
Silty soil

Action Make raised beds. Do not double dig.

- Few worms/worm channels.

Action Lime if acid. Add organic matter. Improve drainage if needed. Dig to relieve compaction.

- The hole that you have dug collects water, which stays for a few days.

Action Improve drainage on the site.

- Water sits on the soil surface after rain.

Action Dig soil to reduce compaction. Add organic matter to improve structure. On heavy clay, make raised beds.

How acid or alkaline is it?

The acidity, or pH, of the soil affects its fertility; the ideal level is between 5.5 and 7. Never lime the soil without measuring the pH first, either by using an amateur kit or by sending a soil sample for professional analysis. Ground limestone will raise the pH, whilst organic matter will reduce it slightly. A general idea of soil pH can be gained from the plants growing in your garden (see below).

Is it short of plant foods?

Look at plant growth on the plot. A vigorous crop of weeds indicates a fertile soil; sickly growth indicates that something is wrong. On an empty plot sow a quick-growing green manure (see page 34) to give an indication of fertility.

Poor growth can be caused by poor structure and/or a shortage of plant foods. A professional soil analysis, preferably an organic one, will identify any problems and is well worth the money on a new site. Never add fertilizers 'just in case', as an excess can be as bad as a shortage. Correct major deficiencies with slow-release rock minerals, supplemented initially by faster-acting organic composts and fertilizers.

For further details on this subject see the companion volumes in this series, *Soil Care and Management* by Jo Readman, and *How to make your Garden Fertile* by Pauline Pears.

Plant indicators of acid soil

Blue hydrangea *Azalea*

Plantain *Sorrel*

Plant indicators of alkaline soil

Dianthus *Pink hydrangea*

Spinach *Buddleia*

Clearing a weedy site

There are many ways of clearing weeds organically, the only method not used being weedkillers. Weedkillers do not only kill weeds; they can have far-reaching effects on the environment, including wildlife, soil organisms, people and pets.

- **Forking over, removing perennial weeds by hand** This is hard work, but it produces fairly quick results if done thoroughly. However, the ground may need a second going over. Dig really weedy ground over roughly to turn in the weeds, then leave it for a week or two before forking it over and removing the weeds by hand.

- **Rotavating** This can be a good way of clearing a large area of land infested with perennial weeds, but as it has to be done several times the land can be out of action for a couple of months. Rotavating breaks up perennial weed roots, each bit of which can regrow. Each time the land begins to look green it should be rotavated again. The weeds should give up after the third or fourth pass. The best time to rotavate is in spring and summer, when the soil is not too wet. Rotavating should never be used as a regular method of weed control, as it will eventually break down the structure of the soil.

- **Digging over, turning in the weeds** This can be a satisfying way to produce a clean looking plot quickly, but it is only suitable if you have adequate topsoil. Do not mix topsoil with subsoil. Perennial weeds must be buried 15cm down to discourage regrowth. Do not strip off the top turf as it contains all the goodness. If you must, then remove it and stack it up to decompose for reuse.

- **Mulching** Plants, including weeds, need light to grow. Deprive them of this by covering them with a light-excluding material and they will die. Suitable materials include carpet (hessian backed), and cardboard or newspaper held down with bricks, soil, hay, straw, or logs. Black plastic may also be used, but as it is not biodegradable it is the least acceptable material in an organic garden. The time taken to clear the land will vary, depending on the weeds present. Grass with annual weeds will be cleared in a month or two in spring and summer. Perennials such as bindweed and couch grass can take up to two years. Mulching is best started in the spring or summer when the weeds are growing well.

- **Mix and match** Unless you are prepared to wait several months, or even years, before you can use the land, it is often best to use a combination of digging and mulching. The whole area can be mulched to begin the clearing process, and you can then dig individual beds as time allows, safe in the knowledge that the weeds in the rest of the plot are not getting out of hand.

If the site is growing creeping perennial weeds, such as couch grass, buttercups and bindweed, then it pays to get rid of them from the whole plot before laying out the beds. If the plot you are converting to beds does not contain creeping perennial weeds, e.g. an old lawn, then the pathways can be covered with mulches to clear the weeds, while the beds are dealt with in whichever way you choose. Leaving the paths undug, so the soil is firm, saves a lot of raking and levelling later.

Mulch materials for clearing ground include (from left to right): carpet; black plastic; flattened cardboard cartons

Four newly constructed beds. If you wish to use a wheelbarrow, then do not place your edging across the paths!

Choosing your beds

Although gardening on a bed system is often known as 'raised bed' gardening, beds do not have to be raised, they can be almost flat. It is also called 'deep bed' gardening, but beds do not have to be deeply dug, they can be run on a no-dig regime. This section will help you to decide which sort of beds are the best for you.

No-dig

No-dig gardening is gardening without turning over the soil. It is a common misconception that soil must be dug over before plants will grow in it. After all, nature has never had any trouble! The HDRA runs a flower and vegetable garden that was converted from grass pasture without any digging at all. Six years on, it is still growing well. The soil has a good strong texture and the topsoil is fine and crumbly.

There is often concern that a soil that is not dug will become compact and airless. As long as it is fed with compost and other organic materials, as all soils should be, this should not be the case. On a no-dig system these materials are spread over

the soil surface and are gradually taken into the soil by worms and other creatures. Their activity creates a good strong soil structure in which roots will thrive.

The top few centimetres of a no-dig soil develop a particularly good structure, so that seedlings find it easy to emerge and rain can easily penetrate the soil. There is no worry of a hard cap forming.

Applying plant foods to the surface also keeps them where they are of most use. The majority of soil microbes – the creatures responsible for making plant foods available – live in the top few centimetres of soil, and this is where most of a plant's feeding roots will be.

More manure?

Many advocates of a no-dig system insist that it requires much more in the way of compost, manures and organic mulches than other growing systems. This need not be so. The HDRA has run successful no-dig gardens for many years, using almost exactly the same inputs as for a dug plot. The only added extra has been a hay or straw mulch for the potatoes. Do not be put off no-dig by thinking that you cannot make a sufficient compost.

15

To dig or not to dig?

NO-DIG

Advantages

- Better for your back.
- Protects soil structure, especially on light soils.
- Makes a good, stable soil structure.
- Makes a friable topsoil through which seedlings emerge easily. Soil less likely to cap.
- Keeps fertile topsoil in its right place.
- Reduces moisture loss.
- Does not bring weed seeds to the surface to germinate.
- Worms like no-dig systems.

Disadvantages

- Some people like digging.
- Does not expose soil pests to predators.
- Takes longer to improve poor soils.
- Does not deal with compaction and hard pans.

no-dig will not solve compaction problems

worms like no-dig

DIGGING

Advantages

- Breaks up compaction and hard pans.
- Kills annual weeds and surface-rooting perennials.
- Exposes soil pests to predators and cold weather.
- Quickest way of clearing weedy ground.
- Dug soil warms up more quickly in the spring.

Disadvantages

- Hard work.
- Can only be done when the soil is in a suitable condition.
- Destroys soil structure.
- Not suitable where the topsoil is very thin.
- Increases loss of moisture from the soil.
- Raises soil level of beds, so edging boards may be needed to contain it.

digging can be back-breaking

digging exposes soil pests to predators

Which crops?

Most gardeners are used to growing fruit and flowers without regular digging, but vegetables are seen as a different matter. In fact, all vegetables can be grown on a no-dig system. Seeds are sown in drills made in the soil as usual, and plants are transplanted into trowel holes. Instead of digging a trench for runner beans, a thick mulch is used.

The only major difference occurs when growing potatoes. A crop of carrots, for example, can be harvested with little soil disturbance, but potatoes really do have to be dug out. For a totally no-dig system they can be grown on the soil surface, under a mulch. If this is not practical, then they can, of course, be grown in the conventional way. There is no need to stick slavishly to one method of growing if it does not suit you.

Making a no-dig bed

Once the ground is weed-free (see page 14), making a no-dig bed is simple. If it has been disturbed, then rake the soil level. Spread any manure, compost or other required soil amendment over the surface and start growing.

If, when looking at your soil profile (see page 12), you identified a hard pan or compacted soil, then the soil should be dug once or twice before converting to no-dig.

Digging

There is nothing inherently wrong in digging as long as it is done when the soil is just moist, not too dry or wet, and it is not done too often. Excessive digging destroys soil moisture and fertility as it mixes air into the soil, which speeds up the decomposition of the organic material it contains.

Making a 'dug' bed

New beds may be 'single dug' except where there is compaction or a hard pan, in which case double digging is recommended for the initial preparation.

- **Single digging** Dig the soil over to a spade's depth, or the depth of the topsoil, whichever is shallower.
- **Double digging** This involves digging the soil to a spade's depth (or the depth of the topsoil if shallower), then loosening the lower layer with a fork.

Whichever form of digging you use, remember that the aim of the bed system is to avoid walking on the soil. Dig from the path if you can, or stand on a board placed on the soil that you have yet to dig.

If rock minerals and liming materials are to be added, then these can be sprinkled over the soil surface. They will then be mixed in as you dig. Manures, composts and other fertilizers should be added once the digging is complete. They can be hoed or forked into the top few centimetres of soil.

Shaping the beds

Once a bed has been dug it will stand proud of the surrounding soil, especially if the soil is on the heavy side. If it is only slightly raised, then the soil can usually be raked quite easily into a shallow mound shape. If the soil is raised more than a few centimetres, then shape it into a flat-topped mound. The shaping and preparation can be quite rough with widely spaced crops such as potatoes or brassicas. With closer crops the beds need to be well prepared right up to the edges or you will waste a lot of growing space. If you find that the soil is too raised to be able to achieve a flat-topped mound, or if the edges crumble in the first rainstorm, then some form of edging should be used to contain the soil (see pages 19–21).

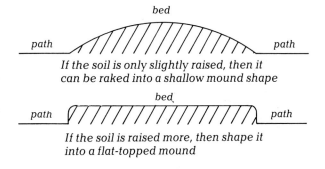

If the soil is only slightly raised, then it can be raked into a shallow mound shape

If the soil is raised more, then shape it into a flat-topped mound

In future years

No-dig

Some gardeners will dig a 'no-dig' garden every four years or so; others will not. There are no set rules, and the gauge should be the performance of your plants.

Digging

There should be no need to double dig a bed more than once or twice. Then, single digging should suffice. As the soil improves, you should be able to prepare it for sowing and planting simply by hoeing it over and then raking it level.

Raised or flat?

Raised 'by default'

Beds tend to become raised above the level of the surrounding paths because:

- Digging mixes air into the soil, so it takes up more space. The effect is most noticeable on medium to heavy soils.
- Paths are compacted by walking on them, so they tend to sink.
- Organic materials such as compost and manure make the soil more bulky.

This sort of bed is fine for most situations. It is preferable for light, well-drained soils where any deliberate raising only makes the soil drain even more easily.

Deliberately raised

Beds can be deliberately raised above the surrounding soil and this can be beneficial:

- Where the topsoil is thin, over a poor subsoil.
- Where drainage is poor.
- On a heavy soil where raised soil will warm up earlier in the spring.
- Where any reduction in the amount of bending required is a blessing!

Raised beds should have a permanent edging to keep the soil in place (see pages 19–21). The soil is raised by double digging (if appropriate) and then adding extra topsoil and composted materials. Soil can be taken from the paths, and more can be brought in if the existing topsoil is very thin. Leaf mould, shredded bark and other soil conditioners can also be added, as well as any manures and composts.

Gardeners who cannot get down to the soil can bring the garden up to their level by creating brick-built beds, which are raised 60cm or more. For more information on constructing this type of raised bed consult books or organizations concerned with gardening for the disabled.

Beds which have been raised 'by default'

Beds with edgings of coping stones, and wide gravel paths

Edgings and paths

Having chosen the type of beds that you are going to make, the next stage is to decide upon the edgings and paths.

Edging the beds

I once heard a lady say that she could not afford to have a bed garden because of the expense of the wood that was needed to make the edges. In fact, beds do not have to be surrounded by a permanent edging and the materials used do not have to be expensive.

Benefits of raised edging
- Allows deliberate raising of the bed to get away from poor drainage or subsoil.
- Can make management of beds raised by digging and manuring easier.

- Helps to keep soil off the paths.
- Keeps loose path material off the beds.
- Can look attractive.
- Sturdy edging is good for sitting on!
- Prevents plants at the edges of the beds being trampled by mistake.
- Keeps the shape of the bed well defined.

The height of the edging depends on how much the bed is raised and the materials used. Where a bed is being deliberately raised, something around 30cm is probably appropriate. Where it is raised 'by default', 10–15cm should be sufficient.

Materials for edging
A whole variety of materials can be used to edge beds, from brand new wooden planks and Victorian-style tiles to scrap-wood and old bricks. Your choice will depend on how much you are prepared to pay, what is available locally, how attractive you want the garden to look, the shape

19

of the beds, and how much digging you are going to do. Beds that are regularly dug need a more firmly fixed edging than no-dig beds.

Wood

Brand new wood can be an expensive option for bed edging, but it can look very smart, especially when stained an attractive colour. For small beds, log roll (a roll of half-logs joined together into a strip that can be rolled up) can be used. A cheaper option is to ask at wood merchants for offcuts and other 'waste' timber. Second-hand wood from pallets, railway sleepers or old floorboards can be good value. Slab board, the rough timber/bark strips trimmed off the outside of logs, is available cheaply from sawmills. Long lengths of log, either whole or split in half lengthways, are another alternative.

Wood is easiest to manage when used for straight edges, but it can be curved to some extent. It is easy to fit, as it can be nailed or screwed to short posts which have been hammered well into the ground. Fix the edging strips to the outside of the posts if possible, so that you do not trip over them and they do not get in the way when laying paths. A useful tip, if you use a hose to water the beds, is to have corner posts standing 30cm or so above the ground to prevent the hose being dragged across the plants.

A bed of lettuces with an edging of wooden boarding, and a gravel path

Temporary edging

If you do not have enough wood to edge all of the beds, then use the edging for the closely spaced crops which are often sown from seed, e.g. onions, carrots, beetroot and salads, and move the edging around the garden with these crops. It can easily be fixed temporarily, by hammering in posts either side of the planks every 2–3m or so.

Temporary edging

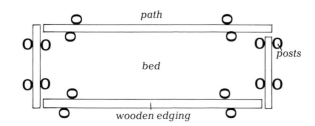

Wood preservatives

Ideally, wooden edging should be left untreated, and replaced as necessary. If this is not acceptable, then use a preservative based on natural ingredients, or use one that acts as a water repellent. At the very least, use one that is harmless to plants. Creosote is too hazardous to use in an organic garden.

Bricks, tiles, slates, etc.

Rounded concrete curb stones can be cemented in to give a solid permanent edging. Victorian-style edging tiles or frost-resistant bricks can look attractive, and they fit well around irregular shaped beds. They are best on beds where little digging is to be done, as they are easily disturbed.

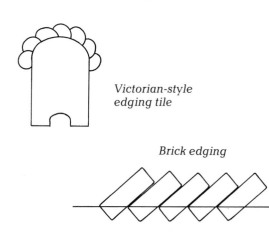

Victorian-style edging tile

Brick edging

A bed of chives and garlic chives surrounded by a brick path

A bed of lettuces surrounded by a carpet and wood-chip path

A bed of radish seedlings with an edging of logs, and a path of wood chips

A bed of red orache and other herbs with an edging of coping stones, and a gravel path

Paths

With a bed system there is quite an expanse of ground which is officially designated as 'path'. This can be managed in various ways.

Paths may be left simply as bare earth which is hoed to keep the weeds down. These are cheap and easy to make, but are time-consuming to maintain and not very ornamental. At the other end of the scale are brick or paving paths, which can look very attractive. They are more expensive and complex to make, but, when laid well, are easier to maintain and have a long life span. In between the two extremes there are mulched paths, which are quite simple to make if you can find the materials. These will need varying amounts of maintenance work every year and vary in their life span, cost and appearance.

The chart describes a selection of path-covering materials and their characteristics, but you may well come across more. In the organic garden, biodegradable natural materials are preferable to plastics.

A bed of attractant plants (Californian poppy and nemophila) with a path of concrete slabs

A bed of tagetes with a woven plastic path

Path-covering materials and their characteristics

Material	Cost	Ease of construction	Ornamental value	Suitability for odd shapes	Life span	Weed-controlling ability	Edging needed?	Remarks
Bare earth	Cheap	Simple	Low	High	Long	Bad	No	
Grass	Cheap	Simple	High	Low	Long	Good	No	High maintenance, as regular mowing and edge trimming needed.
Newspaper under hay/ straw	Cheap	Simple	Low	Medium	1 year	Good	No	May increase slug problems in some situations.
Sawdust	Cheap	Simple	Low	High	1–2 years	Average	Yes	Must be kept topped up to around 10cm to maintain weed control.
Spun polyester fibre topped with wood chips/home shreddings or sawdust	Average	Average	High	Medium	10 years	Good	Preferably	Keep covering of wood chips, etc., topped up.
Woven plastic	Average	Average	Low	Medium	3 years	Good	No	Cover with wood chips/sawdust to increase life span.
Second-hand felt underlay, hessian-backed carpet	Cheap	Average	Low	Medium	2–3 years	Good	No	Keep in place with wire staples.
Paving slabs, bricks	Expensive	Complex	High	Low	10 years or more	Good	No	Good weed control if laid well on a good foundation. A layer of spun polyester fibre underneath also gives good weed control.
Gravel	Average	Complex	Medium	Low	Long	Average	Yes	A good foundation is needed to prevent weeds becoming a problem. A layer of spun polyester fibre can be used.

Growing on beds

Planning

Before you start to grow anything, it is a good idea to take some time to think about your needs and wants. If required, then the first step is to allocate space for perennial plants, e.g. shrubs, fruit, herbs, etc. These are grown in the same way as on a conventional plot. Advice on choosing fruit for a bed garden can be found on pages 44–46.

Annual plants – vegetables, herbs and flowers – will fill the rest of the garden. Their spacing and layout can be very different from a conventional plot. This section, together with the crop-by-crop vegetable chart on pages 36–43, will help you to plan, sow and plant.

Vegetables

Make a list of the vegetables that you want to grow and sort them into family groups. This will show you which of them need to be kept together in a rotation (see pages 25–27). Within each group, allocate a priority rating to help you decide how much of each to grow and which can be left out if space runs short. Finally, note the period of

time that each crop spends in the ground, so that a succession of cropping can be worked out.

Flowers and herbs too

Add to your list some attractant flowers, to bring colour and useful pest-eating creatures to the garden (see page 33), and any other annual flowers and herbs that you want to grow. These can be grown on separate beds, or mingled with the vegetables (see page 32).

Spacing

The crop-by-crop vegetable chart (see pages 36–43) details plant spacings for individual vegetables and, together with the spacing chart on page 28, will help you to work out how much space you need for each. For herbs, flowers, and any vegetables not included in the chart, use the 'between plant' spacings normally recommended.

Does it all fit?

You may have to adjust your plans to fit the space available and to keep within the limits set by crop rotation. A simple way to do this is to cut out pieces of paper to represent the area that you want for each crop, using the same scale as your garden plan (see page 6). For example, imagine that you would like to grow sixty medium-sized onions. The spacing chart on page 28 shows that, at a spacing of 15cm between plants, 1m of 1.25m wide bed will accommodate them. Cut out a piece of paper to represent 1m of bed, mark it 'onions', and stick it on your plan (using a non-drying glue to allow for repositioning). Do this for every crop until you have filled up the beds, remembering to refer to the section on crop rotation as you go. If everything fits, fine! If not, then the crop areas can easily be trimmed to fit.

It is worth making a second plan for crops that are to follow on, including fertility-building green manures.

Crop rotation

The basic principle of crop rotation is that plants of the same botanical family, which are prone to the same soil-living pests and diseases, should not be grown in the same spot every year, but should be moved around the garden. The aim is to help prevent the buildup of problems in the soil, such as club root, white rot and eelworm, which often have no other means of control. Because crops have different soil requirements, a rotation also makes sure that each area of ground has, approximately, the same taken out and put back into it over the period of the rotation.

Planning a rotation

In Britain, the crops that make up the bulk of a standard gardener's vegetable plot tend to be potatoes, peas and beans, roots, onions and the cabbage family, so it is these families that make up the framework of a traditional rotation. However, there is no need to stick to this format if, for example, corn, pumpkins and courgettes, beans and onions are the major crops in your garden. As long as you follow the principles of rotation the choice is yours. The crops in each family, which

A four year crop rotation

VEGETABLE FAMILIES

Alliaceae	*Chenopodiaceae*	*Cruciferae*	*Cucurbitaceae*
ONION	BEETROOT	BRUSSELS SPROUTS	CUCUMBER
GARLIC	SPINACH	CABBAGE	COURGETTE
LEEK	SWISS CHARD	BROCCOLI	MARROW
SHALLOT	SPINACH BEET	CALABRESE	SQUASH
		CAULIFLOWER	PUMPKIN
		KALE	
		RADISH	
		SWEDE	
		TURNIP	
		MUSTARD	
		KOHLRABI	

Leguminosae	*Solanaceae*	*Umbelliferae*	*Miscellaneous*
PEA	POTATO	CARROT	Plants that are fitted in where space permits. They do not have to be kept with any other plants in particular.
BROAD BEAN	TOMATO	PARSNIP	CHICORY AND ENDIVE
FRENCH BEAN		PARSLEY	JERUSALEM ARTICHOKE
RUNNER BEAN		SCORZONERA AND SALSIFY	CORN
ALFALFA		Although more closely related to lettuce, these are usually grown with root crops.	LETTUCE
CLOVER		CELERY AND CELERIAC	PHACELIA
TARES		Although these belong to the *Umbelliferae* family, they require very different conditions and are usually grown separately.	GRAZING RYE
FENUGREEK			
TREFOIL			
LUPIN			

should be kept together in a rotation, are listed above.

The order in which crop families follow each other in a rotation tends to be governed by their particular soil requirements. Potatoes, for example, prefer an acid soil so they are grown as far away as possible, in time, from any lime application. In effect, this means liming (if required) immediately after the potato crop has been lifted. Both the pea and bean family and the cabbage family appreciate some lime and so could follow potatoes. You should also try to alternate light and heavy feeders, the light feeders relying on the leftovers of manure and compost applied to the others. So, potatoes are followed by peas and beans which provide their own nitrogen. Onions fit in nicely with peas and beans in a rotation; some extra compost can be supplied to them if needed.

One example of the order in which the major crops can follow each other on a plot is:
● Potatoes, followed by legumes and onions, followed by brassicas, followed by root crops, with potatoes returning after four years – making this a four year rotation.

Other combinations are quite feasible:
● Cucurbits, followed by peas and beans, followed by brassicas, followed by roots and onions.
● New potatoes and tomatoes, followed by peas and beans, followed by salad beets and celery, followed by corn and courgettes.

The longer a crop rotation lasts, the better. Eight to ten years is ideal if the space is available; four years is a more practical figure for most gardens. Divide the vegetable garden up into 'sectors' of equal area, one for each year of the rotation. Each sector may be made up of more than one bed, and, in fact, a rotation can be easier to manage if this is the case. If you cannot achieve equal areas, then the quantity of each crop family that you can grow will have to be adjusted accordingly each year. The constraints of a rotation system may mean that you have to trim your plans for certain crops so that they do not take up more space than that allotted to their particular family. Because crops are sown, planted and harvested at different times of the year, families may overlap at times, e.g. for a while winter broccoli may be growing in the same bed as peas.

Green manures should also be included in crop rotation plans. If you want to grow one that is related to a crop, then grow it straight after the crop rather than before. One combination to avoid is winter beans and broad beans as these are very closely related; both are varieties of the same bean *Vicia faba*. Green manures can be used to extend a rotation. A bed can be put down to a green manure for a season, or a year, or more. This will rest it from cropping and improve fertility and structure.

If you are growing a very mixed garden where a formal rotation is not practical, then at least try to follow one plant with another that is not related to it.

Always keep a note of what is grown on each bed each year, as this makes future planning much simpler!

Strawberries
Strawberries are a difficult crop when it comes to rotation. They are best replaced after three crops, as after this their vigour declines and virus,

Strawberries growing in a bed, with a mulch of woven plastic

disease and pest problems increase. It is possible to grow a plot of strawberries in each sector of a three or four year rotation, planted a year apart.

If virus or aphid attacks are common, then it is preferable to remove the old plants before planting the new, to avoid rapid transfer of pests and diseases. One way to manage this is to set aside three beds for strawberries, which could be included in the vegetable area or perhaps at the base of wall-trained fruit. The first bed is planted up in late summer/early autumn to crop the following year (year 1); these plants are taken out after cropping in year 3 and the second bed is planted up that autumn, and so on. In the mean time, the other 'strawberry' beds can be used for overspill vegetables from the main rotation; early potatoes fit in before planting strawberries, and leeks can be planted after the strawberries are taken out in year 3. Salads, flowers and green manures can also be grown.

Spacing and layout

The recommended spacing for vegetables can vary quite dramatically, from seed packet to gardening book to garden 'expert', and it can be quite difficult to determine which is right. In fact, they all may be, because in reality the correct spacing is that which produces a good crop of vegetables of the size that you require, and this will not be the same for everyone.

The effect of spacing
Within limits, the more space that you give a plant, the larger it will grow, but, except for show purposes, few people really want giant onions and cabbages like footballs. As plants are moved closer together the size to which each one will grow is reduced, but as more plants can be fitted into the same space total yields actually go up.

However, there does come a time when a further reduction in spacing becomes counter-productive; hundreds of plants may be fitted into a square metre of ground but none will have sufficient room to grow what you want to eat.

The spacings given for different vegetables in the chart on pages 36–43 are those that have been found effective at the HDRA. They are given simply as a basis for you to work from and to adapt to your own situation. On soils where food and water may be limited, wider spacing than that suggested may be necessary to achieve success. This may also be wise in damp regions, where fungal diseases are a regular feature; more space between plants allows better air circulation which discourages the spread of disease. Economics can

Onions show well the effect of spacing on size

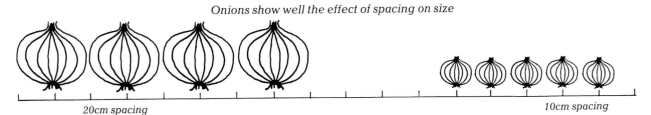

20cm spacing   10cm spacing

also play a part, e.g. where seed potatoes or onion sets are concerned. A closer spacing may give a higher total yield but this has to be balanced against the greater number of sets or tubers required.

The following chart gives an approximate idea of how many plants can be grown on a metre length of bed, according to the spacing used.

Spacing in centimetres	Number of plants per metre of 1.25m wide bed	Layout
5	580	offset
7.5	246	offset
10	139	offset
15	60	offset
20	35	offset
22	26.25	offset
25	22.5	offset
30	16	offset
40	7.5	square
45	6.75	square
60	3.2	square
75	2	staggered
90	1.5	staggered

The effect of layout

In a conventional garden vegetables tend to be grown close together within each row, with a greater distance between the rows. As plants naturally grow equally in all directions, the result of this uneven layout is competition between plants in the row, with plenty of wasted space between the rows, in which weeds can grow.

Row layout

shaded area = competition between plants

On a bed system there is no need to leave space to walk between rows, and a more even distribution can be used. Modern research has proved that spreading plants evenly over a bed makes much more productive use of space. In this type of layout, described as 'offset', each plant is an equal distance from all the plants around it and,

therefore, only one figure is needed when calculating plant spacing.

Offset layout

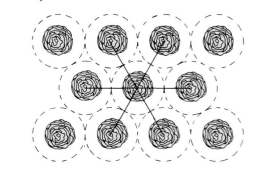

├─────────┤ = *recommended spacing*

Once the space between plants exceeds 30cm, more plants can be fitted onto a 1.25m wide bed if they are not offset but are planted 'on the square'. This means that each plant is now further from some than from others. The spacing can be reduced slightly to compensate for this.

Square layout

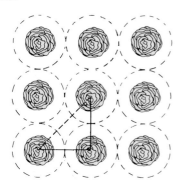

if ├─────────┤ = *recommended spacing*,
then ├─ ─ ─ ─ ─ ┤ = *slightly more than this spacing*

At even wider spacings, when there is only room for one plant across the width of a bed, the plants are arranged in a 'staggered row' up the bed.

Staggered layout

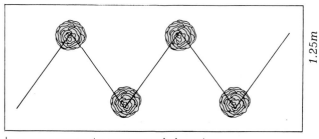

├─────────┤ = *recommended spacing*

Weed control

One disadvantage of even spacing, which you may encounter with the more closely spaced crops, is that it can make hoeing impractical. However, the advantage of this type of layout is that it gives the quickest production of a weed-suppressing cover of crop foliage over the bed, so a single hand weeding before the leaves meet may be all that is required for many crops.

Sowing and planting

When sowing and planting, there are various methods which can be used to achieve an even spacing between the plants.

Stations or rows?

Station sowing is perhaps the simplest way to get an even spacing with directly sown crops, seeds being sown where individual plants are required. With small seeds, two or three are usually sown at each station and then thinned later to one seedling. In the case of larger seeded crops, such as peas and beans, one or two seeds at most are sown at each station, to reduce the quantity of seed required. 'Spares' can be sown in between stations, to transplant into any gaps.

Station sowing can be very time-consuming for closely spaced, small seeded plants such as carrots. The alternative is to sow these in conventional rows and then thin to the final layout. The spacing between the rows can be slightly smaller than that recommended for between the plants.

Transplants are simply planted out at the required spacing.

Sowing in rows

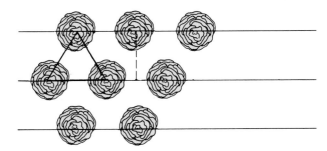

if ├───────┤ *= recommended spacing,*
then ├─────┤ *= slightly less than this spacing*

Measuring up

To get the most out of a bed, measure the space between plants quite accurately, so that the maximum number of plants are fitted onto the bed. After a little practice, this can be done using a stick cut to the appropriate length, or, if you want to be even more accurate, a triangular template. The following example describes how it is done.

Spacing stick. This can vary in length from 7.5cm to 90cm, depending on the crop being planted.

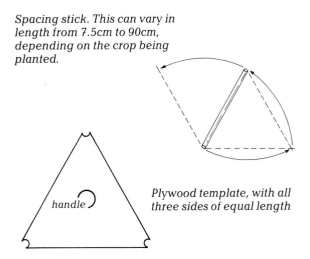

handle

Plywood template, with all three sides of equal length

Planting onion sets at 15cm spacing

1. Measure 7cm in from the end of a bed and stretch a line across.
2. Plant sets along this line, starting 10cm in from the edge and using a stick cut to 15cm to measure the spacing.
3. Use the stick to position the second row of sets equidistant from the first.

When sowing or planting up a whole bed, it is quicker to plant the first row along the length of the bed and work from there.

If you find this method difficult, then there is nothing wrong with marking each row or every second row with a string, reducing the distance between rows slightly as explained earlier.

No-dig

Seeds are sown in the same way as on a 'dug plot', either in drills (formed in the usual way) or station sown. If the soil is not light enough to press the larger seeds into, then a small trowel hole can be made at each station. Because manures and composts are put on the surface of a no-dig bed, the top few centimetres of soil usually have a lovely friable structure through which seedlings find it easy to make their way.

Plants are transplanted into trowel holes as usual. For further information on planting individual crops, see the chart on pages 36–43.

Multi-sowing

Space for raising plants indoors is usually in short supply. One way of saving space is to 'multi-sow' in divided trays or modules, raising several plants in each division of the tray. Each little clump of plants is transplanted as though it were a single plant, using a slightly wider spacing, and all the seedlings are left to grow, with no thinning. This technique can be used for beetroot, carrots, leeks, onions and turnips. The end result is not, as you might imagine, a clump of stunted vegetables, but a healthy cluster of medium-sized roots. Some varieties suited to multi-sowing are listed in the table; it is well worth experimenting with others.

Crop	Possible varieties	Number of seeds per module	Spacing
Beetroot	Early ones such as Boltardy.	2 'clusters'	30cm
Carrots	Round-rooted types, e.g. Rondo.	7	23cm
Leeks	King Richard, Titan.	6	30cm
Spring/ pickling onions	White Lisbon, Paris silverskin, Purplette.	6	15cm
Onions	Hygro, Robusta.	6	30cm
Turnips	Early White Milan.	6	30cm

Although this technique moves away from the basic idea of plants evenly spaced over the bed, it can be extremely useful and productive. The wider spaces between clumps of plants can be used for intercropping.

A bed of multi-sown onions with a path of stone slabs

Intercropping and mixed planting

Intercropping

Intercropping is the practice of using the empty space between plants, whilst they are small, to grow a quick crop of something else. It is an invaluable technique for getting the most out of a limited space. For example, summer radishes can be sown between parsnips and will be ready to harvest before they start to crowd the parsnips. Salads are ideal for intercropping. Some are small, so they are unlikely to compete with other plants; some grow fast, so they can be harvested before slower crops get started; others are shade tolerant, so they will thrive between taller crops.

Intercropped cabbages and lettuces. Note the protective mats of carpet underlay around the cabbages, and the paths of carpet and stone slabs.

Intercropping is easier to manage on a bed system than in a conventional garden because:

● The even layout of plants leaves neat gaps to be filled in.

● The space between plants is not needed for standing on.

● It is easy to reach between plants on a narrow bed.

Priorities are important with intercropping; there is a main crop, which can be a flower, fruit or vegetable, and a minor crop, the intercrop. It is important to remember which is which, so that the minor crop is not allowed to flourish at the expense of the main crop, which can happen if the timing is not quite right. If the minor crop is getting out of hand, then remove it.

In this book, the division into main and minor crops is used to distinguish intercropping from mixed cropping/planting and companion planting, although all three techniques do overlap to some extent and may be given slightly different definitions by other gardeners.

---

1. Plants suitable for being intercropped
Usually slow to start, and/or of upright habit, and/or widely spaced.
Parsnips
Leeks
Multi-sown onions
Dwarf peas (in rows)
Brussels sprouts
Broccoli
Kale
Winter cabbage
Sweet corn
Half-hardy annuals, e.g. French marigolds

---

2. Plants suitable as intercrops
Usually compact, and/or quick growing, and/or with upright habit, and/or shade tolerant.
Lettuces, small
Carrots, round rooted
Radishes, summer
Spring onions
Turnips, summer
Landcress
Corn salad
Early beetroot
Kohlrabi.
For a quicker return, transplant where possible rather than sowing direct.

Good combinations

Not all the plants in box 1 are suitable for being intercropped with those from box 2; the right combinations have to be selected to ensure a good return from both. Some suggestions are given in the chart on pages 36–43. Both crops must have sufficient space, light, fertility and moisture to develop. If you are doing a lot of intercropping, then you may find it necessary to increase the amount of compost (or any other material) that you add to the soil. Widening the spacings between plants of the main crop can also be helpful, but do not overdo this or the benefit of intercropping will be lost.

Companion planting

Companion planting is the deliberate growing of one plant with another to protect one of them from pests or disease. Books listing scores of 'good companions' are available. In theory, the idea is excellent, but practical advice on how to grow the companions together, and evidence that particular combinations work, is sorely lacking. Undoubtedly, companion planting can work, but it can also fail miserably so it is best tried with caution.

Mixed planting

Quite recently, there has been a move back to the cottage garden tradition of mixed planting, that is, growing fruit, vegetables, flowers and herbs all together to make a garden that is both attractive and productive. This style of gardening is well suited to the smaller gardens of today, where there is little room to separate the fruit, vegetable and flower gardens. It also suits organic gardening, as pests are less likely to get out of hand when there is a good, diverse mixture of plants.

Initially, it may seem rather strange to grow, for example, lettuces in a flower bed, but there are so many attractive varieties available these days that they do not look out of place. Once you begin to forget the rigid divide between vegetables and flowers, it is amazing what can happen. Carrots start to be valued for their attractive foliage and nasturtiums for their edible flowers.

The ultimate expression of mixed planting is to have everything – annuals, perennials, root crops, flowers, herbs, leafy vegetables, etc. – all jumbled up together. If you can get it right, then this can be most effective. However, to keep this sort of garden looking good, new plants must be ready to go in as soon as others are removed, and a watchful eye is needed to make sure that certain plants are not overwhelmed by their neighbours. It is also more difficult to keep up with soil treatments and rotation.

An easier system to manage is one where the vegetables that are grown in any quantity are kept together in their own beds, with annual flowers and herbs added for colour and diversity. The delight of a bed system is that it is so easy to intersperse the more functional beds with ornamental ones where flowers and/or herbs and/or fruit can be grown. For good measure, a few vegetables can also be added. Half-hardy annuals can be intercropped with lettuce, parsley makes a striking bedding plant, and poppies stand out beautifully against the grey-green foliage of a summer cabbage.

Salad crops fit in particularly well in a more ornamental garden. Lettuces are now available in plain or frilly, and red or green, varieties. Endives also have frilly varieties, and chicories can add a splash of colour to a bed. Some of the oriental mustards, e.g. Mizuna, have an attractive deeply cut leaf, whilst chervil produces a mass of fine feathery leaves.

Mixed planting. This bed contains a mixture of herbs, flowers and fruit.

Plants for pest control

The activity of beneficial insects, that is, insects which will help to control pests, can be increased by growing flowers which provide them with food (often in the form of pollen and nectar) and shelter. The more food they have, the greater the number of offspring these useful creatures will produce to carry on the good work. When planning a garden, whether mixed or not, always include some of these flowers.

Plants that have been shown to support beneficial insects

These plants and varieties have been shown to support beneficial insects; others may also do so.

ANNUALS	BIENNIALS	PERENNIALS
Poached egg plant *Limnanthes douglassi*	Carrot *Daucus carota*	Tansy *Tanacetum vulgare*
Phacelia *Phacelia tanacetifolia*	Parsnip *Pastinaca sativa*	Golden rod *Solidago* spp.
Californian poppy *Eschscholzia* spp.		Clover *Trifolium* spp.
Sunflower *Helianthus annuus*		Angelica *Angelica archangelica*
Buckwheat *Fagopyrum esculentum*		Shasta daisy *Chrysanthemum maximum*
Cosmos *Cosmos bipinnatus*		Pearl everlasting *Anaphalis* spp.
Tagetes 'Lemon Gem' *Tagetes signata*		Globe thistle *Echinops* spp.
Annual convolvulus *Convolvulus tricolor*		Sea holly *Eryngium*
Dill *Anethum graveolens*		
Candytuft *Iberis* spp.		

Phacelia

Parsnip

Tansy

Some useful creatures and the pests they eat

Creature	Predator or parasite?	Pests eaten
Lacewing larvae	Predator	Aphids, thrips, mealy-bugs, moth eggs, scale insects, mites, caterpillars.
Ladybird adults and larvae	Predator	Aphids, mealy-bugs, spider mites, soft scale.
Hover-fly larvae	Predator	Many species of aphid, including greenfly and blackfly.
Tachinid fly larvae	Parasite	Many species of caterpillar and sawfly larvae.
Parasitic wasp larvae	Parasite	Codling moths and caterpillars, aphids, root flies, scale insects.

A summary of maintaining your beds

Soil fertility

For further information see the companion volumes in this series, *How to make your Garden Fertile* by Pauline Pears, and *Soil Care and Management* by Jo Readman.

Fertility is not just a question of plant foods, it is also to do with a good structure that provides the right balance of air and water for plant roots and soil microbes. • **To improve soil structure** Do not dig unless you must. Grow green manures. Add as much organic matter as possible; dig it in, or leave as a surface mulch. • **To increase the amount of food available to plants** Improve soil structure to release reserves in soil. Grow green manures. Add organic composts and manures, but do not overdo it. Use rock minerals to correct deficiencies. Use organic fertilizers to supplement the above if required. • **Soil improvers** *For soil structure (organic matter)*: leaf mould; green manures; straw; shredded bark; cocoa shells; coir; proprietary soil conditioners. *For structure and plant foods*: garden compost; well-rotted manures; hay; mushroom compost; seaweed; proprietary manures and composts. *For plant foods*: rock minerals; blood, fish and bone; bone meal; hoof and horn; worm-casts; proprietary organic fertilizers. • **Recycling** One of the basic rules of organic gardening is to recycle plant foods within the garden, and to use 'renewable' resources, such as manure, as far as possible. This stops wastage and pollution. *Compost*: convert kitchen and garden waste, supplemented by brought-in materials such as animal manures, into garden compost. A worm compost bin may be more suitable for small gardens with little to compost. *Leaf mould*: collect fallen leaves in the autumn, water well if dry, and store in plastic sacks or a wire mesh cage until rotted down. *Animal manures*: strawy horse and cattle manure should be stacked up to decompose before use, or added to a compost heap. Do not use manures from intensive farms, as they may be contaminated with additives fed to the livestock.

Green manures

For further information see the companion volume in this series, *How to make your Garden Fertile* by Pauline Pears.

Green manures are plants that are grown to improve the soil. They are sown, allowed to grow for a few weeks or months, then chopped down and dug into the soil. • **Green manures** Take up and use plant foods that would be washed out of a bare soil; these are returned when the plants are dug back in. Protect soil structure from heavy rains and prevent erosion. Suppress weeds. Improve soil structure. Varieties such as clover can take up nitrogen from the air, increasing soil fertility. • **Plants for green manuring** Quite a selection of plants can be grown as green manures. Which one you choose will depend on the season of sowing and the period for which it is to be grown. Some, such as buckwheat, are frost-tender fast-growing annuals, suitable for a few weeks cover in the summer. Others, such as clover, are frost hardy and can be left to grow for a year or more if needed. When the ground is needed for use, or when the green manure is beginning to toughen (whichever is sooner) the plants are cut down and dug into the soil. Here the foliage decomposes, and the goodness it contains is released to be used by the plants that are grown next. Because the green manures are still green and relatively tender, there is no risk of nitrogen robbery. • **No-dig** Green manures can be grown on a no-dig system. Instead of being dug in, they are hoed off or cut down and left as a mulch. Clovers, trefoil, and rye, which might regrow, are best cut and covered with a mulch to kill them.

Crop protection

For further information see the companion volumes in this series, *Pests: How to control them on fruit and vegetables*, and *Healthy Fruit and Vegetables*, both by Pauline Pears and Bob Sherman.

Cloches and covers of various forms can protect plants from adverse weather conditions and from many pests. The French bell jar was the original 'cloche' used on intensive beds, protecting one or two plants only. The modern equivalent of this is the plastic drinks bottle! Propping up individual bell jars to air and water the plants must have been a time-consuming job. Fortunately, modern materials which allow air and water through to the plants make life easier. The increasing popularity of the bed system of growing means that it is now possible to buy cloches, covers, etc., to fit a 1.25m wide bed.

● **Types of cover** *Plastic bottles*: use to protect young plants from the weather, flying pests, rabbits and slugs. *Cloches*: cloches that cover the full width of the bed afford protection to a large number of closely spaced plants. Those covered in a material that allows air and water to penetrate are easier to manage and are also more effective pest barriers; as soon as a cloche is opened up, pests can get at the plants. *Frameless covers*: fine lightweight materials, often known as 'fleece', can be laid directly over plants to protect against weather and pests. Very fine mesh netting may also be used in this way, without requiring a framework.

Weed control

For further information see the companion volume in this series, *Weeds: How to control and love them* by Jo Readman.

The close spacings used on a bed system mean that leafy crops may need only a single weeding when they are small to keep them weed-free. As soon as their leaf canopy covers the soil few weeds are able to penetrate it. Other crops, that require wider spacing or have narrow leaves, may need to be weeded more often or treated with a mulch. ● **Methods of weed control** *Hand weeding*: because the soil is not walked on it remains relatively uncompacted, making it easy to pull out weeds by hand. *Hoeing*: the more widely spaced crops can be hoed, preferably on a dry day when the young weeds will soon die. If you wish to hoe all crops, then adjust the recommended spacing so that there is sufficient space to hoe between the rows. Decrease the 'in row' spacing to compensate. *Surface mulches*: weed growth can be suppressed by the use of surface mulches, either spread around the plants or laid over the bed and planted through. Suitable materials include newspapers, hay or straw, manure or compost, and grass mowings. *Green manures*: if a piece of ground is to be left bare for a few weeks or more, then a green manure can be grown to smother out the weeds. *Crop rotation*: this ensures that the same weeds are not encouraged in the same spot every year. *No-dig*: weed growth should be much less on a no-dig bed where the soil is not disturbed.

Watering

For further information see the companion volumes in this series, *Soil Care and Management* by Jo Readman, and *Healthy Fruit and Vegetables* by Pauline Pears and Bob Sherman.

The most efficient watering system is rain. Improving soil structure will make sure that the water soaks into the soil rather than running off the surface and ensure that the soil holds on to as much as possible without getting waterlogged. Covering damp soil with a surface mulch will help to keep it moist. ● **How much?** Young seedlings and transplants must have enough water to get established. After that, regular watering in dry weather is not always necessary. Some crops need watering only in the very driest of seasons; some will benefit from extra water at a particular stage of growth; others will only really do well if they are never short of water.

● **Make the best use of water** Water into pots or plastic bottles sunk into the ground next to individual plants, so that the water goes straight down to the roots. Do not use a sprinkler: use a handheld hose, can, or trickle system. Apply a reasonable quantity (at least 10 litres per sq m) at one time. Only water the plants that you want to grow, not the weeds as well. Do not water plants that can survive without.

Crop by crop – growing vegetables on a bed system

FAMILY	CROP	VARIETIES FOR BEDS	SPACING AND LAYOUT (see pages 27–29)
Alliaceae	**Garlic** *Allium sativum*	No special recommendations.	*Bulbs* 10 – 15cm. *Leaves* 5cm. LAYOUT Offset.
	Leek *Allium porrum*	No special recommendations.	*In seed-bed* 4 × 15cm. *In final site* 15cm for medium-sized leeks and 10cm for small slim ones. LAYOUT Offset.
	Onion *Allium cepa*	Robusta and Buffalo for multi-sowing, see page 30. Spring and pickling varieties for intercropping. Purple-skinned varieties for extra ornamental value.	*Spring* Sow broadcast in 8cm wide bands, with 30cm between the centre of each band. Alternatively, sow thinly in rows 7cm apart. Multi-sown blocks: 15cm. *Pickling* 7cm. Multi-sown blocks: 15cm. *Maincrop* Sets/plants 10–20cm, depending on size of onion preferred. Use the wider spacing where white rot or mildew is a problem. Multi-sown modules: 25–30cm. *Japanese* Sow 2.5 × 22.5cm in autumn. Thin to 10 × 22.5cm in spring. Multi-sown modules: 25cm. LAYOUT Offset.
	Shallot *Allium cepa*	No special recommendations.	20cm. LAYOUT Offset.
Chenopodiaceae	**Beetroot** *Beta vulgaris*	For intercropping and multi-sowing, choose a quick early variety. In an ornamental garden, yellow varieties and those with dark foliage provide added colour.	*Early* 13cm. *Multi-sown* 22cm. *Maincrop* 15cm. *Small roots for pickling* 7.5cm. Early crops should not be planted closer than this as competition between plants makes for later cropping. Vary the spacing to produce the size of roots that you require. LAYOUT Offset.
	Spinach *Spinacea oleracea*	No special recommendations.	25cm. LAYOUT Offset.
	Spinach beet and chard *Beta vulgaris cicla*	Swiss and Ruby chard are very ornamental; the latter has a tendency to bolt early.	22cm. LAYOUT Offset.
Compositae	**Chicory and endive** *Cichorium intybus* and *Cichorium endiva*	A selection of very ornamental green and red, and plain and frilly, varieties are available. Some are grown to produce a head, others are sown broadcast to cut when 5–8cm high.	*Heading varieties* 15–30cm (chicory), 25–40cm (endive). *Broadcast cutting crop* 1cm. LAYOUT Offset.

Harvest when leaves begin to turn yellow in mid/late summer. If they are left until the leaves have died back, then leaves and bulbs separate.

NO-DIG Loosen soil with fork before harvesting garlic bulbs.

Lettuce, lamb's lettuce and other small salads can be grown between transplanted leeks.

In dry areas, prepare the leek bed in spring if possible. Digging the land over in summer dries it out at a time when rainfall is low anyway.

NO-DIG Multi-sown leeks do not require any digging, see page 30.

Spring onions can be fitted in between many larger crops. Multi-sown spring onions can be planted between multi-sown maincrop onions.

Keep onions well weeded.

Red onions

Harvest when leaves turn yellow. Shallots store for much longer than onions.

NO-DIG Loosen with a fork before harvesting by hand.

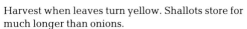

Early varieties, raised in modules and picked young, between sweet corn or winter brassicas. Attractive foliage for interplanting in ornamental beds.

Leeks

Summer spinach prefers some shade in hot weather, so it can be grown between taller crops, provided that there is enough moisture.

Attractive foliage for planting in ornamental beds.

Less prone to bolt than spinach. Will tolerate light shade.

Chicories and endives are different forms of the same plant. They are generally easy to grow and trouble-free. Can be eaten raw in salads, or cooked.

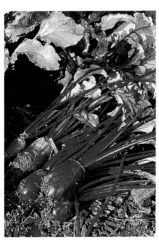

Beetroot

37

FAMILY	CROP	VARIETIES FOR BEDS	SPACING AND LAYOUT (see pages 27–29)

Compositae
continued

Lettuce
Lactuca sativa

A wide selection is available for growing all year round; red or green, plain or frilly. Can be very ornamental. For a quick crop, some varieties can be sown broadcast to cut when 5–8cm high.

Heading and loose-leaf varieties: 15–30cm (depending on variety). *Broadcast cutting crop* 1cm. LAYOUT Offset.

Cruciferae

Broccoli, sprouting
Brassica oleracea var. *cymosa*

No special recommendations.

60cm. LAYOUT Square.

Brussels sprouts
Brassica oleracea var. *gemmifera*

No special recommendations.

Dwarf varieties 55cm. *Tall varieties* 75cm for picking over a period. *Small sprouts for once-over picking* 60cm. LAYOUT Square.

Cabbage
Brassica oleracea capitata

Small, compact varieties make better use of space and are more practical in use than the larger-headed ones.

This depends very much on the variety used and the size of head required. Closer spacing gives smaller heads, so adjust it to suit.
Spring cabbage 30cm, or 10 × 30cm thinning out finally to 30cm each way. Use thinnings as 'spring greens'. *Summer cabbage* 30 – 45cm. *Autumn/winter cabbage* 38 – 45cm.
Spacing can be adjusted slightly to fit maximum number of plants on a bed.
LAYOUT Offset (spring), square (summer, autumn/winter).

Calabrese
Brassica oleracea var. *cymosa*

No special recommendations.

15 – 30cm. At the closer spacing, plants will tend to produce a main spear only and will all be ready to pick at the same time. LAYOUT Offset.

Cauliflower
Brassica oleracea var. *botrytis*

No special recommendations.

For summer use 60cm. *For autumn use* 60cm. *For winter use* 75cm. *For spring use* 75cm. LAYOUT Square (for summer and autumn use), staggered (for winter and spring use).

Kale or borecole
Brassica oleracea acephala

No special recommendations.

45cm. LAYOUT Square.

Radish
Raphanus sativus

Quick summer varieties are useful for intercropping.

Summer varieties 5cm (small). *Winter varieties* 20cm. *For pods* 60cm. LAYOUT Offset (summer and winter varieties), square (for pods).

Turnip
Brassica rapa

Quick-growing varieties are useful for catch cropping and intercropping.

Quick varieties 15cm. *Maincrop* 20cm. LAYOUT Offset.

Lettuce is a useful, quick catch crop or intercrop. Will tolerate some shade in summer.

Transplant between rows of early peas. Intercrop with quick summer cabbage, lettuce, landcress, etc.

Firm soil gently before planting if it has been dug recently. The plants grow large and may need to be staked to prevent the roots being disturbed when rocked by the wind. Earthing up the stems to encourage extra rooting can also help.

Transplant between rows of early peas. Intercrop with quick summer cabbage, lettuce, landcress, etc.

Firm soil gently before planting if it has been dug recently. The plants grow large and may need to be staked to prevent the roots being disturbed when rocked by the wind.

Lettuce

Small summer varieties can be grown between wider spaced winter brassicas. Their grey/green foliage is a perfect foil for orange, red and yellow flowers, such as poppies, in an ornamental garden.

Increase spacing on dry sites where there could be a soil-water shortage.

Cabbage

See broccoli, above.

Firm soil gently before planting if it has been dug recently.

Summer radishes are quick enough to grow between carrots, parsnips and other root crops, if sown at the same time as the main crop.

A crop of small summer turnips can be fitted in between peas, winter brassicas or broad beans.

Broccoli

FAMILY	CROP	VARIETIES FOR BEDS	SPACING AND LAYOUT (see pages 27–29)
Cucurbitaceae 	**Courgette and marrow** *Cucurbita pepo*	Bush varieties are easier to manage on beds than the trailing types.	*Bush·varieties* 60cm. *Trailing varieties* 60–90cm. LAYOUT Square or staggered (depending on spacing).
	Pumpkin and winter squash *Cucurbita pepo* and *Cucurbita mixta*	Bush varieties are easier to manage than the more vigorous trailing ones.	*Bush varieties* 60cm. *Trailing varieties* 75–90cm (depending on variety). LAYOUT Square (bush), staggered (trailing).
Gramineae 	**Sweet corn** *Zea mays*	No special recommendations.	30–45cm. LAYOUT Offset or square (depending on spacing).
Leguminosae	**Broad bean** *Vicia faba*	Dwarf varieties can be useful as they do not need to be supported and can be intercropped when young.	25–30cm. LAYOUT Offset.
	French bean *Phaseolus vulgaris*	Climbing varieties are better where slugs are a problem. Dwarf varieties with coloured pods are easier to pick, as the pods stand out well against the foliage.	*Dwarf varieties* 15cm. *Tall varieties* 15 × 60cm. LAYOUT Offset (dwarf), double row (tall).
	Pea *Pisum sativum*	'Leafless' varieties can be grown in a block across a bed. Because most of the leaves have been reduced to tendrils, they support each other without the need for sticks or netting.	To fit the principles of bed-system growing, peas should be spaced evenly over the ground. This is only practical for short early varieties and leafless ones, which require a spacing of 7.5cm. *Early and maincrop varieties* 5cm each way in a triple row, 30–40cm between rows. Grow in rows either across or up the middle of the bed. The former is really only practical if pea sticks are used for support. LAYOUT Offset (short early and leafless), row (early and maincrop).
	Runner bean *Phaseolus coccineus*	Dwarf varieties create less shade than taller ones. In an ornamental garden, choose tall varieties for flower colour; red, red and white, white, or pink.	*Dwarf varieties* 25cm. *Tall varieties* 15 × 60cm. Grow tall beans, supported by canes, in a double row along the middle of the bed. They can also be grown up a wigwam of canes, but this does not give such an efficient use of space. LAYOUT Offset (dwarf), double row (tall).
Rosaceae	**Strawberry** *Fragaria* sp.	No special recommendations.	Two rows per bed, 38–60cm between plants, depending on soil and variety. LAYOUT Row.

Use the initial wide space between these plants to fit in some quick beetroot, lettuce, etc.

Alternating bush and trailing varieties on one bed can make better use of space.

Use the initial wide space between these plants to fit in some quick beetroot, lettuce, etc. Trailing varieties can be directed through a sweet corn crop.

Pumpkins and marrows can be allowed to trail through corn. Salad plants, such as Mizuna, that take light shade, can be grown between the corn. Alternatively, sow trefoil (a green manure) that will grow through the winter once the corn has been cut down.

Corn cobs should be picked when tassels are brown and the seed exudes a milky juice when punctured. For full flavour, eat raw or lightly cooked within ten minutes of picking.

Squash

Quick crops, such as radish or lettuce, between dwarf beans.

Tall varieties may need support. Suspend a strip of wide-mesh pea/bean netting horizontally over the bed when the plants are young so that they grow through it, or make a similar sort of network with string.

Fill up space around tall bean crops with annual flowers, lettuce, small cabbage or other small plants.

Short varieties can be spaced so that tall winter brassicas can be planted between the rows, ready to grow away as soon as the peas are finished. Grow short flowers or vegetables either side of a single row up the middle of the bed.

Sweet corn

Fill the remaining space around beans with annual flowers, lettuce, dwarf French beans or other small plants.

When watering in dry weather, the water may run off the bed rather than soaking into the soil. When planting a double row of tall beans, make a shallow dip between the rows to water into, or sink plant pots into the soil along the rows for the same purpose.

NO-DIG Although it is traditional to dig deep trenches for runner beans, they grow well on a no-dig system. Once plants are growing strongly, mulch the soil to keep it moist.

NO-DIG Plant as usual.

Strawberries

FAMILY	CROP	VARIETIES FOR BEDS	SPACING AND LAYOUT (see pages 27–29)
Solanaceae 	**Outdoor tomato** *Lycopersicon lycopersicum*	Low-growing bush varieties which sprawl over the ground and need no staking. Tall varieties may also be grown.	*Bush and tall varieties* 45 – 60cm, depending on variety, and fertility of ground. If two rows are grown along a 1.25m bed, then use 40cm spacing within each row. LAYOUT Square.
	Potato *Solanum tuberosum*	Very large tubered varieties do not suit the close spacing of a bed system.	*Earlies* 30cm. *Second early and maincrop* 30–37.5cm. Plant tubers in individual planting holes. These spacings will produce a good crop of medium-sized potatoes. If possible, buy seed potatoes where you can 'pick your own'. Choose the smaller tubers which are more suited to close spacing, as each produces fewer stems than a larger one. As each stem is equivalent to a plant, small tubers give a more even distribution of plants over a bed, with less likelihood of greening (which occurs when overcrowded tubers are pushed to the surface). Small tubers are also cheaper. LAYOUT Offset (earlies), square (second early and maincrop).
Umbelliferae	**Carrot** *Daucus carota*	Choose 'early' short-rooted varieties for intercropping.	*Short-rooted varieties* 15cm. *Maincrop varieties* Station sow at 15cm, or sow in rows 20cm apart thinning to 5–8cm in the row. LAYOUT Offset.
	Celeriac *Apium graveolens*	No special recommendations.	30cm. LAYOUT Offset.
	Celery, self blanching *Apium graveolens*	Self-blanching varieties are much easier to grow than the 'trench' varieties. They are best grown in a block, which suits the bed system.	15–25cm. The wider spacing gives heavier plants with thicker stems. Always plant in a block for good blanching of stems. LAYOUT Offset.
	Parsnip *Pastinaca sativa*	No special recommendations.	10–20cm, depending on variety, and size of root required. A smaller-rooted variety, grown at 10cm each way, should give roots up to 5cm in diameter. LAYOUT Offset.
Valerianaceae	**Lamb's lettuce** *Valerianella locusta*	No special recommendations.	*Sown broadcast or in rows* 10cm. Eat thinnings.

Quick small crops can be grown between young tomatoes.

Tomatoes

Mulch young potato plants with old hay, grass, etc., as an alternative to earthing up, which is not possible with close spacing. If small tubers are planted, then this should not be necessary. Take extra care when harvesting a closely spaced potato crop. The soil is so full of tubers that it is easy to damage some. Closely spaced plants produce a lot of foliage, which may need to be tied in to prevent it smothering neighbouring beds.

NO-DIG There is nothing against planting potatoes in the conventional way on a no-dig bed. They will have to be dug up at harvest, but this is quite acceptable unless you want to leave the soil totally undisturbed. Potatoes can be grown without any digging; planted on the surface under several layers of mulch which are added during growing.

Carrot fly can be repelled by growing a row of carrots between four rows of onions. Ornamental foliage.

Firm recently dug soil gently before sowing; small seeds do not germinate well in the light, fluffy soil. If soil is dry, then water bottom of the seed drill before sowing.

NO-DIG Carrots can produce excellent crops on a no-dig system; shorter-rooted varieties may be more successful on heavier soils. The soil may have to be loosened with a fork before harvesting.

Potatoes

Will appreciate some shade from taller, neighbouring crops in high summer, but must not dry out.

Mulch plants once they are growing well. Water when possible in a dry year.

Will appreciate some shade from taller crops in high summer, but must not dry out.

Water when possible in dry weather. A 'fence' of sacking or black plastic around the block of celery will ensure that the outer plants are also blanched. Alternatively, surround with a border of an upright annual flower.

Radishes sown between station-sown parsnips, at the same time, will be ready to harvest before they start to compete with the slower-growing parsnips.

NO-DIG Sow as usual. Loosen roots with a fork before pulling up. Shorter varieties may be more suitable for no-dig beds on heavier soils.

A useful winter intercrop.

Sown in autumn, it will stand a harsh winter. Mild flavour.

Celeriac

Blackberries, boysenberries, loganberries and similar soft fruit can be grown against a fence

Fruit beds

Fruit growing is now within the bounds of most gardeners, even if the garden is small and the family moves house every five years or so. Modern fruit breeding programmes have produced varieties of tree and soft fruit that are more compact, and much quicker to start cropping, than in the past. For example, apple trees that grow to only 1.8m and produce their first crop in only two years make a great change from the giants of the past that were only worth planting as a long-term investment.

Fruit is traditionally grown in its own area, kept apart from the flowers and vegetables. Where bird protection is required this is quite a practical way of organizing it, but there is no reason why fruit should not be grown in a bed garden along with everything else. After all, it can look most attractive; pear and cherry blossom in the spring, strings of redcurrants glistening like fabulous jewels in the summer, and the stylish look of trained fruit trees in the winter.

If fruit is to be included in a bed garden, then it must be kept compact, so that it does not outgrow its bed or cast too much shade. A combination of

Rootstocks

A fruit tree is made up of two varieties; the fruiting variety, which is grafted on to the rooting variety, or rootstock.

The rootstock has a considerable effect on the final size of a tree. The same variety of apple, for example, can be reduced from 10m to only 2m merely by changing the rootstock. The more dwarfing stocks also encourage earlier cropping. In most cases, both root and fruit varieties are the same type of fruit; pears are the exception, being grafted on to quince rootstocks.

Rootstocks that will produce compact trees, suitable for a bed garden, are listed in the table.

new varieties, appropriate rootstocks, and traditional training methods make this quite possible.

Using the boundaries

Much use can be made of boundary fences and walls to grow fruit, which can be trained flat

Soft fruit

Type	Forms for small gardens	Aspect (full sun is preferred, if possible)	Final height (depends on variety)	Spacing (depends on soil and variety)	Time to first crop	Notes
Blackcurrants	Bush	West	0.9–1.5m	1.5–1.8m	2 years	Choose a compact variety.
	Hedge			0.75m		
Red/whitecurrants	Bush	North	1.2m	1.5m	2 years	Will require netting against birds.
	Fan		1.82m			
	Cordon single		1.82m	30cm		
	Cordon multi		1.82m	30cm/stem		
Gooseberries	Bush	East/north	1.21m	1.2–1.5m	2 years	Choose upright varieties for small gardens.
	Standard		Variable	1.2–1.5m		
	Cordon single		1.8m	30cm		
	Cordon multi		1.8m	30cm/stem		
	Fan		1.8m	2m		
	Espalier		1.8m	2m		
Blackberries	Trained along wires or over arches	East/north	Depends on wires	3–5m	2 years	Too vigorous for small gardens. Netting required.
Hybrid berries, e.g. loganberries		West				
Raspberries	Single row	Full sun for at least half the day	1.8m	45cm × 1.5m	2 years	Run rows north/south if possible. Netting required.
	Pillars					
Strawberries	See vegetable section					

Tree fruit

Type	Forms for small gardens	Rootstock (assumes reasonable soil)	Aspect (full sun is preferred, if possible)	Spacing (depends on soil and variety)	Final height (depends on variety)	Time to first crop	Pollination notes
Apples	Cordon	M9/M26	South-east	75cm × 2m	Not applicable	2 years	Apples need to be pollinated by another apple to crop. Grow at least two trees which flower at the same time, unless there are other apples nearby.
	Dwarf bush	M27		1.5–2m	1.6m	1 year	
	Espalier	M9/M26		3.5m	Not applicable	2 years	
	Ballerina	MM106		60cm	2.4m	2 years	
Pears	Cordon	Quince C	East or west	45–60cm	2.5–5.5m	3–4 years	Some are self-fertile, but all crop better when pollinated by another variety.
	Espalier			3–4.5m			
	Fan			3–4.5m			
Plums and gages	Bush	Pixy	East facing (cookers only)	3.5–4.5m	2.5m	3–4 years	Some varieties are self-fertile.
	Fan	St Julien A		4.5–5.5m		4–6 years	
Cherries	Fan	Colt	North (acid varieties only)	4.5–5.5m	2.5–3m	3–4 years	Acid varieties, and some sweet varieties, are self-fertile. Must be netted against birds.
		Inmil		3–3.5m			

against wires in fan, espalier or cordon form. Apples, pears, cherries, gooseberries, and red and whitecurrants, can be grown in this way. For success, choose the type of fruit to suit the aspect of the fence (see the table on page 45). Trained fruit takes up very little depth, so flowers, herbs or even vegetables can be grown beneath it once it has become established.

In the garden

In the central area of the garden, posts and wires can be erected to take trained fruit. These will create slim fences to break up the plot. Raspberries and blackcurrants do not like being tied into a fence or wall, but modern blackcurrants will fit neatly into a 1.25m bed, grown either as individual bushes or more closely spaced to form a hedge. Raspberries can be grown in a single row as a tall hedge, or planted around a central support post (four plants per post) to form a raspberry pillar.

Free-standing fruit can also be fitted into a bed garden, e.g. Ballerina apples take up little space and need no special pruning. Apples and plums can be trained to make compact 'lollipop' shapes. Even untrained apples, on M27, the most dwarfing rootstock, do not grow too large. If you can find a supplier, then standard gooseberries and redcurrants (bushes grafted onto a tall stem) make good feature plants. They are also much easier to pick.

The details in the tables on page 45 should help you to decide what sort of fruit can be grown in your own garden.

Raspberry canes grown in a bed

Glossary

Bed system: a system of growing in which the garden is divided up into narrow beds which are separated by paths.

Broadcast: seed sprinkled thinly over the ground.

Cap: a hard crust on the soil surface.

Catch crop: a fast-growing crop used to fill in temporary gaps.

Compaction: where soil is packed down due to weight from above.

Cordon: a form of trained fruit, often planted at an angle, which consists of a single straight stem with fruit produced on side shoots kept short by pruning.

Cutting crop: a salad crop grown to cut when a few inches high. Two or three cuts can usually be taken.

Double digging: cultivating the soil to a depth of two spits (a spit is the depth of a spade).

Earthing up: heaping earth up around the base of a plant.

Espalier: a form of trained fruit consisting of a central stem from which horizontal fruiting arms grow.

Fan: a form of trained fruit with fruiting arms trained into a fan shape.

Friable: describes a fine, crumbly soil with no hard or wet lumps.

Green manure: a plant that is grown to benefit the soil.

Mulch: any material spread over the soil.

No-dig system: a system of growing that avoids any turning over of the soil.

Organic: a method of growing plants which avoids the use of chemical pesticides and artificial fertilizers.

pH: a measure of the acidity of the soil. A pH of 7 is taken to be neutral; a soil with a pH of less than 7 is said to be acid, while a pH figure of more than 7 is said to be alkaline.

Rootstock: a plant which provides the roots for another variety of the same plant, which is grafted on to it.

Seed drill: a narrow, shallow depression made in the soil, by the edge of a rake or other tool, for sowing seed into.

Soil pan: a hard layer below the soil surface, often only 30–45cm below the surface.

Index   Chapter headings are in bold type